Input/Output

Change Your Environment, Change Your Life

Moses Pierre-Paul

Copyright © 2020 Moses Pierre-Paul

All rights reserved. This book or any portion thereof may not be reproduced or used in any manner whatsoever without the express written permission of the author except for the use of brief quotations in a book review.

Table of Contents

Preface .... *ii*

Chapter 1 - The Law of Input/Output *1*

Chapter 2 - Environment *4*

Chapter 3 - Changing Your Environment *13*

Chapter 4 - The Process *25*

Conclusion *35*

Preface

It was a beautiful Sunday afternoon while sitting at my mom's dining room table when I got a text message that got me thinking. That morning, I had given the sermon at my church and an associate of mine that heard about it asked me where I learned to become the man I am today. Surprised by his question, the first thing that came to mind was "take the negativity out of your life, and increase the positivity" and so that's that gist of what I told him. Later when I thought about it, I wasn't so sure my answer was helpful to him. But although I might have been vague, my reply wasn't random. Up until then I often wondered why my life turned out different. Even more so since a handful of the people I grew up with have either lost their life, mind, or freedom. How am I different?

During the early part of my life, I lived with my mom, older sister, and little brother in an inner-city area called Bain Town. Bain Town, which is located in the capital of The Bahamas is a low-income area, and my mom who immigrated from Haiti had very little to support my siblings and me. She often shares how at one point our rent was only $7 a week and she could not afford it. Beyond the economic challenges, there were many bad influences and as a naive little boy, I got caught up in many of them. I can still remember throwing glass bottles at kids from another school even though I would have only been in grade 3 or 4.

But something happened just before I turned 9. Due to financial struggles, my mom, little brother, and I moved to the United States to live with my aunt and her family. Although it was for the better, that transition for me had its own series of challenges. Despite them, living with my aunt was a pivotal point in my development. My aunt's home was strict and the discipline I received while living there improved my character. Three years later, we moved back to Bain Town and even though I wasn't the same, I found my way back into trouble.

Bain Town wasn't all that bad, however. I remember the sense of community and looking forward to the weekly opportunity to attend church. Attending church, which was in another area, was similar to living with my aunt in the United States. Each visit, in little ways that I can only now appreciate, made subtle improvements to my mentality over time. Fast forward a few years, I became the youth director, graduated from college, and worked as a freelancer. A few years more, as I'm writing this, I am married to a wonderful woman, live in my own home, and have a rewarding career. What's more, I was honored to be elected an elder at the same church I looked forward to attending each week.

Compared to some people, what has become of my life at the age of 29, isn't that impressive. But considering where I started and had a high probability of ending up, it is far better than I or anyone else could've imagined. This little book is my attempt to share what I believe to be the reason why. If you apply it, I assure you your life will change also. Enjoy!

1 - The Law of Input/Output

There is a simple yet powerful law that exists and is the basis for much of how the world works. You've likely heard or referred to it by another name, but in this book, I'll call it the law of input/output. Pronounced without the slash, I define it as whatever goes into something, determines what comes out of it. Unlike a law that is put in place and enforced by a government, input/output is a natural law. This means it never changes. Just like the law of gravity guarantees that anyone or anything that falls off a building will end up on the ground, the law of input/output has a consistent effect on anyone or anything that meets its criteria.

Input/Output Is Everywhere

You can find the law of input/output at work in every area of life. At times it doesn't seem consistent, but a closer look will always show it is. Take computers for example. If you were to study computers, you will encounter a subtopic that's called input/output. How do I know? I majored in computer information systems, and input/output in computing is admittedly one of the things that inspired this book.

In computing, there are devices classified as input devices, and others classified as output devices. Examples of a computer's input devices are the mouse and keyboard.

They are considered input devices because they are the devices that allow us to insert data into a computer. On the other hand, examples of output devices are monitors and printers. It is through them that data comes out of a computer. In accordance with the law of input/output, computers can only give output in response to what they received as input. In other words, if two different people used a computer in the same way, they can expect the same results. If you don't put anything in, you won't get anything out. Or as you may be familiar, "garbage in, garbage out". Let's look at another area.

You can also find the law of input/output at work in biology. Whether it's a tree, animal, or human being, each looks like what it came from. As a human being, your traits, such as your eye, hair, and skin color came from your parents. Your eyes may look like your mother's eyes and your nose may look like your father's nose. Your parents, in turn, received their traits from their parents and so on. The way a person looks (output) is based on the genetics (input) their parents contributed when they were conceived. Even if you can't point out a child's traits in their immediate parents, you are sure to find it somewhere in their family tree. As you would expect, animals are the same and when it comes to trees, the seeds that come from them grow to become like them.

As a final example, we are all aware of how diet and exercise affect our health. We know that if we are gaining weight, there's a reason for it, and if that reason happens to be diet-related, we make changes in order to see a difference. The reason you can have the confidence that if you change your diet, you'll change your weight is because of the law of input/output. Altering the input of diet affects the output of weight.

Focus On The Input

From the examples I gave in the last section, you may have noticed that each output starts with an input. Because of this arrangement, whenever you want to change a particular output, you should focus on changing the input that caused it. Now you may be thinking that's obvious, after all, I just gave the example of how we know we have to change our diet in order to change our weight. You are correct. But it's only obvious if you're looking at a small part of a bigger picture. If a person's diet is the reason for their weight, the law of input/output dictates that there must also be a reason behind a person's diet. Once we find that reason, there must also be a reason behind it. Each step back eventually points to a primary reason. That primary reason, which is not only the reason behind our diet but also what we become in life, is what we'll explore in the next chapter. As the primary input, it's the input you should focus on if you want to change your life.

2 - Environment

At the end of the last chapter, I showed that in order to change your life, you should focus on changing the primary input that caused it. Let's work our way back to finding that primary input.

Earlier, I shared that the law of input/output is the basis for a person's diet affecting their weight. But weight is only one of the countless results we get in life because of input. What our lives are today is the combination of inputs we received up to this point. Starting from conception, the genetic input from both our parents made us. After birth, and up until a certain age, it is our parent's choices that determine the inputs we receive in life. This input takes the form of the schools they make us attend, what we watch, where we go, and so on. Over time, we start to make more of those decisions for ourselves.

We decide which career path to pursue, which job offer to accept, the type of person we marry if we decide to get married, and the list goes on. Within each of the choices we make are a related set of choices. For example, after choosing which career path to pursue, we have to decide how we will get qualified for that career. If college is required, we have to decide if we're going to get a loan or apply for a scholarship.

Like the choices our parents made for us, each of our choices determine the inputs we receive. Along the way, those inputs translate to outputs that make our lives.

If your life today is the result of the choices you've made or that was made for you up to this point, it also means your life in the next 3, 5 or 10 years will be the result of those choices and the choices you make from now until then. This means, if you want a better life in the next 10 years, you have to start making better choices. The question now is, how to make better choices?

For many of us, making better choices is difficult. Although we know it would make our lives better, somehow that hope alone isn't enough to motivate us. Like eating healthy, we may start off good, but then we find ourselves making bad eating choices again. The reason this happens is because of the point I made at the end of the last chapter. Do you remember? "Whenever you want to change a particular output, you should focus on changing the input that caused it."

Recognizing that the choices we make are the reason behind our actions which in turn determine the state of our lives, the law of input/output states that our choices must also have a reason behind them, and as you now know, behind that reason must be a reason also. Don't give up on me

Input/Output: Change Your Environment, Change Your Life

just yet! This book won't be an endless search for reasons concluding with God or a big bang. I'll get to it before the end of this paragraph. The reason we make the choices we make is because of the way we think. This is why James Allen states in his book As A Man Thinketh, "a man is literally what he thinks, his character being the complete sum of all his thoughts." And what's the reason behind the way a man thinks? I argue it's his Environment.

The Meaning of Environment

In the dictionary, the word environment is defined as "the surroundings or conditions in which a person, animal, or plant lives or operates." In this book, I define a person's environment as the collection of everything that acts as input to their mind. This includes, but is not limited to the information they get from other people, their experiences, and the content they watch, read and listen to.

The Way Our Environment Affects Us

At birth, our minds are like blank computers. Over time our environment installs software on it and that software determines how we operate. Things that we consider to make up our identity such as the language we speak, our culture, and beliefs all come from our environment. In the same way a computer is powerful and capable of doing many things, we are powerful and capable of many things. In other words, we have a lot of potential. Just so we're on the same page, potential is the ability of a thing to do or become something. If that thing never does or becomes what it could have, that doesn't change it's potential. An example of this is a car's ability to go at a certain speed. Regardless of how a car looks or what the speed limit is on the road it's being driven, its ability to go at a certain speed remains the same. That is to say, external conditions don't change its potential.

Another example of potential is a seed's ability to become a tree. Although they may not look so, some of the smallest seeds become some of the largest trees. What's key to note is, like a car going top speed, the thing that determines if a seed becomes a tree, is not the seed itself. It's the environment surrounding the seed. If you were to place a seed on the tile in your house, it will never become a tree. Placed outside among rocks and water it sparingly, it may grow a little. But placed in good soil and given sufficient water and sunlight, it becomes a fully grown tree. The seed placed in each of those environments is the same seed. What becomes of it is based on the environment it is placed in. It is the seed's environment that triggers what's inside of it to come out. The extent to which it comes out depends on what its environment is capable of nurturing.

Our environment affects us the same way it affects a seed. We all have potential and the extent to which we reach that potential is based on our environment. If you were to review the life of any person you consider to be successful, you would discover that they did not become successful in a vacuum. You would see that their environment over the course of their life brought out of them who they are today. This is the point Malcolm Gladwell makes in his book Outliers. In writing about how successful people became the success that they are, he argued that "we should look at the world that surrounds the successful—their culture, their family, their generation, and the idiosyncratic experiences of their upbringing". This is probably the reason why Bill Gates, one of the examples Malcolm uses, often describes himself as lucky. In the same way, a person's success in life points to their environment, a person's lack of success or life in general points to their environment. Hence why it's what we should focus on. Let's look at a couple more ways our environment affects us.

Environment Affects What We Believe

Earlier, I indicated that one of the things we get from our environment is our beliefs. Those beliefs are not just limited to spiritual or religious beliefs, but also our beliefs about ourselves and the world. In addition to getting our initial beliefs from our environment, every other input we receive is filtered through it and builds upon it. Starting off with the wrong beliefs can have a snowball effect, leading a person down a path that's difficult to change. Belief is the reason why two people can see the same thing and each of them interpret it differently. You may have heard people say that you can either look at a glass of water as half full or half empty. This is not just for one time events that don't meet your expectations. Instead, it represents a way of seeing yourself and the world in every moment. For example, if you were to go to a grocery store and cannot purchase all the food that you need, you may ask one of two questions. "Why is food so expensive?" or "Why can't I afford the food I need?". With the first, you see the problem as something that's out of your immediate control, while the second sees it as something you can control. The first leaves the situation the same and the second leads you to finding ways to afford the food you need.

As for what we believe about ourselves, the beliefs our environment instills in us about who we are and what we can do can keep us from living up to our potential. When I was growing up, some of the beliefs surrounding me were that people are born more intelligent than others and those with wealth were either born into it, lucky, or did something illegal to get it. And so, believing that certain things weren't possible for me, I didn't even try. It was only recently that I developed the belief that I could write a book. Some beliefs instilled in you growing up may be that you are only capable of having a certain type of job or that marriage is or isn't for you; the list is endless. I'm not trying to argue that some beliefs are right or wrong, instead, I want to show that what you believe about yourself affects what you become and that your beliefs are influenced by your environment.

Environment Can Keep Us Stagnant

A few months after my wife and I moved into our home, my mom planted some banana trees in our backyard. When she planted them, they were about 2 feet high with no leaves. As we watered them, they started to show some signs of growth. But after months of watering them and watching their leaves appear, they didn't get any taller. The issue we later determined was not surprising. Most of the space in the yard was rocky, and although the one spot she found to plant the banana trees was not, it was more like sand than good soil. If we had planted them in good soil, they would have done much better than they did. Instead, they had used up all the available nutrients from the sand like soil and stalled.

Like those banana trees, we can all get to a point where our life remains the same. Not getting worse and not getting better. This is not because we don't have the potential to do better (or worse), but because our environment continues to give us the same amount of its influence to keep us where we are.

How Environment Affects Us Is Neutral

The underlying way our environment affects us is neither negative or positive. It is simply the law of input/output at work. Our environment can only give us what it has. Just like peer pressure, although it has a negative connotation, it is not negative nor positive. If your peers happen to be great people, who do great things, peer pressure for you will be pressure to be a great person and do great things. Likewise, when The Bible states that "bad company, corrupts good character," it must also mean that good company will uncorrupt bad character. This leads me to the last and most important point of this chapter.

You Can Change Your Environment

As I've indicated, our environment determines how we think, and how we think determines our choices, and our choices determine our outcome in life. Which means, if we want to change our outcome in life, the focus should be on the primary input, our environment.

The good news is, unlike trees that have to stay in their environment unless a person moves them, we have the ability to change our environment ourselves. If you make your environment better, you will make your life better. Now let's look at how you can do that.

3 - Changing Your Environment

Jim Rohn once said, "If you don't like how things are, change it! You're not a tree." He was one of the inspirations behind what I shared at the end of the last chapter. That is, we have the power to change our environment so that our lives become better. But since earlier I defined a person's environment as "the collection of everything that acts as input to their mind," you may be wondering what does it mean to change your environment?

What It Means To Change Your Environment

Changing your environment is not something you can do once, forget it and get immediate results. Like nurturing a seed, it's a process that requires consistent effort to see results. Here are a few examples of what changing your environment is like. They are not perfect, but they'll help you get the picture.

Replacing Software On A Computer

Earlier when I shared how our environment affects us, I compared each of us to computers, stating that we all have potential, but the software we get from our environment determines how we operate. The thing about computers is, if you want to replace the software on it with something better, you must first uninstall the old software, then install the new software. But here's what you may not know happens behind the scenes. Uninstalling the old software doesn't get rid of it completely. The computer simply marks the space it took up as available to be overwritten. With the right tools, it can be recovered. As the new software is installed it overwrites the old. So with us, as we change our environment the new input will start to overwrite the input we already have. In the beginning, we will still have some of the old, but over time it will be replaced with the new.

Washing Shampoo Out of Your Hair

Some time ago, there was a video I watched online that showed people who were trying to rinse out their hair get frustrated because someone continued to add shampoo to it. Confused about why the shampoo wasn't coming out, these individuals continued to rinse frantically. Eventually, they recognized that someone was intentionally adding shampoo to their hair causing their frustration. You can imagine their reaction. In this example, hair is like our minds. Water is good input, and shampoo is bad input. The goal is to have hair that is thoroughly rinsed, free from any shampoo. Stop the flow of water and the shampoo takes over.

Replacing A Cup of Dirty Water With Clean Water

The last example I take from The Compound Effect by Darren Hardy. Imagine a cup full of dirty water. By continually pouring clean water into the cup, eventually, all the dirty water gets pushed out. Our minds are the cup, the dirty water represents the state we are in and the clean water is where we want to be. The pouring of the clean water into the cup symbolizes the process of changing our environment and since there is no such thing as an empty cup of water, the desire is to keep it clean. Now that you have a good idea of what it means to change your environment, let's transition into practical ways of doing so.

Your Change Strategy

Knowing What You Want Your Life To Be

Deciding you want your life to change is the first step to having a changed life. The second step is deciding what you want it to be. Deciding is not as simple as one might think. In many cases, we only know we want it to be better. I'll share the solution to that next. For now, if you do figure out what you want your life to be, then you can use what I call the "baking a cake" method. There isn't anything special about my use of a cake. It could also be the "cooking the rice" or "making the salad" method. Like any meal, a cake is baked using a specific set of ingredients and each ingredient has a specific link to the end result. Some ingredients common to all cakes are eggs, flour, water, sugar, and a rising agent. Beyond these ingredients, if you want to make a specific type of cake, like a chocolate cake, then you would use chocolate cake ingredients specifically.

When you know what you want it to be, changing your life is simply a matter of finding the environment that will give you the ingredients to become it. For example, if you know you want to be a better communicator, then your environment should consist of things that will contribute to improving your communication skills. This may include attending public speaking classes, watching professional speakers present, and researching speaking techniques. With the baking a cake method, you select the right environment to put yourself in by assessing it's s ability to give you the ingredients required to become what you want to be. Here's an example from my experience.

There was a point in my life when I decided to become an entrepreneur. But at the time of that decision, I had an employee mindset. In the beginning, I would completely forget that I made that decision. I would continually research ways to get a better job. Eventually, I started reading books, listening to podcasts, and watching videos on entrepreneurship. In addition to that, I listened less to content related to getting a better job. It was not that anything was wrong with the job-related content, it simply wasn't giving me the ingredients necessary for what I wanted to be. Over time a change occurred and my actions proved that I was thinking less about a job and more about owning a business.

The more you understand what you want your life to be, the easier it is to recognize which environment will or will not help you get there. But like I mentioned earlier, In many cases, we don't know what we want our lives to be. We only know we want it to be better. Let's look at how we can guarantee that next.

Wanting A Change For The Better

Wanting a better life but not knowing in what way is where I believe most people find themselves. How can you accomplish this? Ensure you are getting better input. Any change in your environment that ensures better input than your current environment will make your life better. This was how my life began to change for the better. In the beginning, I never thought I could have a better life so I didn't try. Here's one of my earliest experiences that opened my eyes to the possibility.

While I was in grade school, I was an average student for the most part. During one of my last summer breaks, I had a conversation with one of my teachers and she told me that I or another student made a significant improvement. Knowing the other student and myself, I thought there had to be some mixup. But when I got my report card, somehow, I managed to get a 3.40 GPA. It was my last year in school and I made the honor roll for the first time. I was in shock and believed it was a mistake. Nevertheless, it motivated me to focus on my school work, and the next term I got the same GPA! Later in life, as I reflected on that experience I recognized that my environment had changed. I had developed a greater respect for my teachers, which caused me to pay more attention in class and submit all my assignments.

You may have had a similar experience that showed a change occurred in your life. Like me, you weren't trying to change but upon reflection saw that you did make unintentional changes to your environment causing it. Yes, the law of input/output works even when we're ignorant of it. Now recognizing it's a law, you can intentionally make your environment better knowing that your life, in turn, will be better.

Using Both Strategies

In explaining the two change strategies, you may think that you have to choose one or the other. In reality, both are usually used together. You may want to position yourself to be better in general, and while becoming better you may want to transform specific areas. For the rest of this chapter, I'll expand on practical ways to achieve both.

Eliminate Your Exposure To The Bad

Although your current environment may not be making your life any better, usually not all of it is bad. Some parts of your environment may be good, but like the banana tree getting water and sunlight but having bad soil, the bad parts counteract the effects of the good. If you identify and eliminate your exposure to the bad parts, you would have improved your environment without introducing anything good.

The people that make up our environment is a good example of this. Usually, there are some people in our environment that encourage us, show that they believe we can achieve our dreams and goals, and do what is in their power to support us. People like these are a gift and should be treasured. On the other hand, there may also be people in our lives that discourage us, show that they don't believe we can achieve our dreams and goals, and may even go out of their way to keep us from doing so. Like rocks in good soil, attempting to extend your roots to grow will continually be blocked by them. So to have a better life, eliminate your exposure to negative people.

I used the people in our lives as an example, but since a person's environment is the collection of everything that acts as input to their mind, eliminating your exposure to the bad parts includes other sources as well. Other bad sources include certain songs, videos, pictures, and social media posts. When I first realized this, I took a step by step approach to eliminating the bad parts of my environment. I told my friends and family to stop sending me inappropriate videos, I started unfollowing people on social media platforms that posted negativity. Eventually, I deleted one of my accounts completely. In time I eliminated the radio talk shows which mostly spoke about all that's wrong in society and I stopped watching TV shows that proved the same. Those changes resulted in me having a better outlook in life. I started to see problems as opportunities and with little to discourage me from pursuing my ideas and learning new things, I did and was rewarded accordingly.

Identifying and eliminating the bad parts of your environment regardless of the source will make your life better. Even if you can't get rid of them completely, any reduction will make a difference. Now let's look at how you can build on top of that.

Increase Your Exposure To Good

I mentioned in the last section that by eliminating your exposure to the bad parts of your environment, it will make your life better even if that's all you do. But what would happen if you not only eliminated the harmful parts but also increased your exposure to good? You guessed it! Your life would have an even greater and faster positive change.

While you may be limited in how much you can associate with the existing good people in your life, you can find other good people to surround yourself with. But remember, since our environment is not limited to the people in our lives, you can also get good input through sources such as songs, videos, articles, books, and social media posts, just to name a few. This is what accelerated my change when I was younger. Despite the literal environment I spent most of my life in having more bad influences than good, I found myself in a position that not only reduced the impact that the bad had on me but added good as well. I had no idea what was happening at the time, but again, ignorance doesn't stop the law of input/output from working.

The first thing that reduced my exposure to bad and at the same time increased the good was church. The church itself was not in the same area, but the bus would pick me up along with other kids to attend weekly youth group meetings and Sunday services. If you looked at my life during this time, you would have not noticed the difference it was making in me, but a shift was happening. When my youth pastor started working at the church full time, it increased the amount of time I spent there. So I was able to develop a relationship with the people at church, and it led to me getting the opportunity to record a song I had written. That then led me to get a computer so I could record my own songs at home. With a computer to produce my own songs at home, I had less reason to go outside and be exposed to the negativity in my neighborhood. Learning how to make songs, which led to videos, graphics and an interest in technology increased my exposure to good input that I couldn't get from my neighborhood.

You might find yourself in a similar position. You could limit or eliminate some of the bad parts of your environment but may not have much good from it that you can maximize. Since your environment is not limited to your physical surroundings, it doesn't stop you from getting good input by other means. Read books written by the people you wish you could surround yourself with. Watch videos and listen to music that uplifts and inspires you. The options are unlimited in today's world. I want to end this chapter with a biblical example that shows how timeless this idea is.

In the book of Joshua, when Joshua took over the leadership role after Moses died, God told him to "Keep this Book of the Law always on your lips; meditate on it day and night, so that you may be careful to do everything written in it. Then you will be prosperous and successful" (Joshua 1:8 NIV). God gave him the secret to prosperity and success. If you read it closely, you'll notice that each part of the verse has an input/output relationship. The end result being a life that's prosperous and successful, reading the verse backward highlights how God tells Joshua he can get there. Reworded with emphasis, it states "To be prosperous and successful, you have to be careful to do everything written in The Book of the Law (The Bible at the time). To be careful to do everything written in it, meditate on it day and night, and keep it on your lips." In essence, God was telling Joshua that a life of prosperity and success comes by taking in and continually thinking about the best input that's available, his laws.

At the beginning of this chapter, I mentioned that changing your environment isn't something you can do once, forget it and get immediate results. Using a few examples I showed how it's a process. Regardless of how you're trying to change, the process requires consistent effort to see results. In the next and final chapter, we'll look at the process. It will give you an idea of what you can expect and serve as motivation to keep you going.

4 - The Process

Changing your environment, in order to change your life is a process. It doesn't happen overnight and the time it takes to see results can be discouraging. When I first went through the process, the time it took didn't matter because I wasn't trying to change and so was unaware of what was happening. Since I discovered that it was a law and started applying it intentionally, it became challenging at times. What I share in this chapter will give you an idea of what you can expect as you go through the process.

Signs That You're Changing

One of the most discouraging parts of the process is not noticing the results. In the early stages, this is probably the reason most people give up on the idea. Like a seed they've planted and started to water, after a few days of not seeing any signs of growth, they stop. When we don't see the results, it's easy to conclude that it doesn't work. But remember, input/output is a law. It always works. Every change in input no matter how little makes a difference. In time we'll see signs that indicate the process is working. Let's look at some of them.

Your Perspective of Others Change

When your life starts to change, your perspective of others starts to change. The people that you saw as accomplished may appear less so. This isn't necessarily because they are, it's because you have grown. To better illustrate this, think of yourself as a little tree that stayed the same size because of the environment. As a small tree, there were taller trees in the distance that you looked up to. But when your environment changed and you started to grow, your perspective of the other trees changed. So during the process, if you are finding fewer and fewer people to look up to, it means that you're growing.

People Will Respond To You Differently

Another sign that you're changing is when people make certain comments about you. In my late teens, I remember working at a photography store and while serving a lady who had a child with her, she made a simple statement that was an eye-opener. When it was time to make the payment, she told the child to "give the man the money". That's it. Why was that simple statement an eye-opener? It was the first time I heard someone refer to me as a man. I had reached a point in my physical growth, and that lady's statement was evidence of it. The same way this happens with physical growth, it happens with mental growth. On another occasion, while talking about a sermon I was preparing, an acquaintance of my sister who only remembered me in my early days made a comment that proves my point. Although years, if not a decade had passed since she last spoke to me, she was surprised that I knew the difference between teaching and preaching. Initially, I was confused by her response, but as I reflected on the incident I recognized that the average person that started where I started probably wouldn't have known the difference. It was a sign that I was different.

In addition to subtle comments, when your life starts to change, people will become increasingly more attracted to you. I remember telling a coworker how sure I was that she was going to be approached for new job opportunities now that she was recently promoted to a manager and completed an industry certification. I told her that in the same way others look at her differently when she's well dressed, her new job title and credentials will make her more attractive. And you know what? She said she was already approached. Because your environment down the line drives what you do, people becoming more attracted to you is a sign that you've changed.

Your Beliefs Change

One of the things I highlighted earlier in this book is that our environment establishes what we believe about ourselves and the world. Because of this, changing your environment will result in a change in beliefs also. Not only do you start to believe you can achieve your goals, but you also start to think about and believe you can achieve things that never crossed your mind. This book is an example. While I had the concept of this book in mind for a great part of my life, it was only within the last few years that I began to think that I could write a book to share it. I'll expand on that development in the next section, but know that it will be the same for you. A new environment expands your world and the better input that comes from it will slowly build your faith. When you see that you are accomplishing goals and dreaming bigger, know that it's because of the changes you made to your environment.

When it comes to the world, your beliefs about how it operates will also change. Instead of thinking that things are simply the way they are, you'll start to recognize the input/output relationship of the circumstances around you and it'll make you realize you have more control over your destiny than you once thought. The filter in which you viewed the world will change. Among other things, you'll see problems as opportunities and failures as lessons learned.

Because you are close to yourself, you won't notice your growth as much as others. It's like when you see a child a few years later and you comment on how much they've grown. To you the change is grand, but to their parent, it doesn't seem so. Not seeing your change doesn't mean you're not changing. Trust that the law of input/output is at work and let the signs you'll see during the process motivate you.

The Process Is Step By Step

Another thing you should know about the process is that it is step by step. In the last section, I mentioned how it was only in the last few years that I began to think that I could write a book. Much earlier than that, during high school my least favorite subject was English and my grades reflected it. When I started college, I was average in my initial English courses. When I got an A- in my last English course because I had been reading more (input changed), it was the early signs of what would come later. In between now and then, after becoming a better writer, it was the process of developing the belief that my ideas would be valuable to others. As my confidence grew, it led me to publish my first set of articles on my blog and now there is this book.

In the process, everything builds on top of the other. You can't get 6 feet tall before you get 5 feet tall. While working to change your life to what you want it to be, don't discount the things you have to go through to get there. Everything you go through builds on top of the other leading you to become what you'll be. That's what happened with David when he took down Goliath. The skill and belief he had he didn't develop on the day of. It was his past experiences that brought him to that point. Look at what David told Samuel when he asked for permission to fight Goliath. "...Your servant has been keeping his father's sheep. When a lion or a bear came and carried off a sheep from the flock, I went after it, struck it and rescued the sheep from its mouth. When it turned on me, I seized it by its hair, struck it and killed it. Your servant has killed both the lion and the bear; this uncircumcised Philistine will be like one of them" (1 Samuel 17:34-36 NIV).

Just like David had to go through the lion and bear to develop the skill and confidence to defeat Goliath, each step you go through in the process of changing your environment will lead you to become and do even greater. This goes hand in hand with the next point.

Changing Your Environment Again

While listening to a presentation of a world-class motivational speaker with a net worth in the 100s of millions, he mentioned how another motivational speaker who was not as financially successful asked him how to earn more money. He was making about a million dollars a year and felt stuck despite his attempts to exceed it. In response, the world-class motivational speaker asked him what was the average income of the professionals he associated with. He replied that they had a similar income to his. That's the issue, the top motivational speaker said. He told him that if he wanted to become a multimillionaire, he needed to surround himself with people who made more money. Given what I shared so far in the book are you surprised by this? You shouldn't be. His environment was not capable of producing the growth in him that he wanted. The solution? Get in an environment that does.

This continues to happen to me and will happen to you too. No, not trying to make more millions each year, but reaching the max of what our new environment has to offer. This is often referred to as entering a new comfort zone. When this happens, you can choose to remain in that environment, receiving the same levels of input that's producing the same output, or you can move to an even better environment in order to have an even greater change for the better. Meeting your goals doesn't mean the law of input/output no longer works. So when you begin to feel stagnant after an initial change, it's time to change your environment again.

You Start To Influence Your Environment

During the process, as your life starts to change, a motivating thing that happens is you become a better part of other people's environments by default. Yes, just like people make up your environment, you make up other people's environment. I can still remember one particular occasion when someone who was new to my environment exposed me to a bigger possibility that changed my life.

During the time I had developed an interest in producing songs and videos, a guy who I knew from the karate classes my brother-in-law taught was at my house one afternoon. Seeing that I was creating music and videos, he told me about a college in the United States that taught the same thing. He even had a brochure from the school with him. At this point in my life, even though I was in high school and walked past a college almost every day, I wasn't quite sure why people went to college. I simply knew it as more schooling that was optional. I didn't know what a degree was and what the benefits were of having one. Anyway, I was excited to know that I could attend a school that would teach me the things I was passionate about at the time. But although I didn't get to attend the college he showed me, that exposure is what led me to earn my associate's and bachelor's degrees.

Before he came around, nobody in my environment had ever talked about college. No one in my household had gone to college. I still remember the doubt in my mom's and older sister's face when I boastfully spoke about my plans to go off to school. On one particular occasion, my older sister who was hoping I would be able to get a job and help my mom with the bills told me to think about a plan B. To this day, I don't blame her. Given the great possibility of being disappointed, I knew she was only trying to protect me. Although she had to help my mom with the bills a little longer, attending and graduating college made me become a better part of her environment. My accomplishment inspired and allowed me to help her earn her associate's degree. What's more? As am writing this, she is 16 credits away from earning her bachelor's!

As your life changes, you'll, in turn, become a change in other people's environments. Imagine how much lives will be positively impacted by yours in the process. Just like that guy inspired me to go to college, and I, in turn, inspired my sister, you'll be an inspiration for many. Isn't that exciting?

The Process Never Ends

If it's your desire to always be better than you are, the process is never-ending. Unlike a car with a built-in speedometer, you have no idea what you're capable of.

Go through the process one step at a time. Let each experience build on top of the other. You'll see the signs that you're changing and the better you will cause a change in others too.

Conclusion

Not long before I wrote this book, I told a coworker that I suspect it will take about a year for me to read all the personal development books I bought on a recent trip. I then said I look forward to the person I will become after reading them all. Recognizing it's the reason my life turned out better, to this day I continue to improve my environment knowing that my life tomorrow will be better because of it.

Take a moment to think about your life as it is today. Can it be better? Of course! Like a seed has the potential to become a tree, you have the potential to become more than you are. All it takes is an improvement in your environment. You have the power to do it. Minimize the bad. Maximize the good. Every change in input counts. Although you may not see the results in the short term, in time you will. Why not start today? A better life awaits!

    Change Your Environment, Change Your Life

Printed in Great Britain
by Amazon